Eric Oduro Wiafe

African Traditional Religion and Christianity's Approach to issues of Marriage and Childbirth

ISBN-13: 978-1456498504

ISBN-10: 1456498509

First Published in December, 2010

The image on the front page of this book is the "Sankɔfa" symbol of the Akan of Ghana. It signifies that Africans should not forget their past (culture and tradition) but must take from the past what is good and use it for their own benefit in the present.
There is also the symbol of the Christian cross in the "Sankɔfa" symbol, and this is to signify the inculturation of African tradition and culture into Christianity so as to make Christianity more tangible, meaningful and practicable to the African.

Contents

iii

Dedication

Dedicated to my departed relatives:

Akosua Tima
Collins Baah
Emmanuel Kwaku Oduro

May your souls rest in perfect peace in the Lord!

Acknowledgements

Many thanks to all my good friends for their
love and support.
May the good Lord richly bless you all.

Prologue

Many African Christians constantly live in a dilemma, and that is, whether to live fully what is enshrined in their African tradition or to live fully their new life in Jesus Christ. This is because there is a strong demand on them to adhere to traditional practices especially, those which are related to life cycle rituals, for instance, childbirth, naming or outdooring and marriage ceremonies. They think that, the references made to the gods, the libation that is poured to the gods and ancestors and the animals that are slaughtered for sacrificial purposes to appease the gods and ancestors during these ceremonies affect their Christian sensibilities. This is because. these are some of the elements in African traditional religion which to them are against their Christian faith and teachings. Much as these Christians want to avoid these practices so as to live in peaceful relationship with other members of the traditional family who may not be Christians, it is a difficult thing to do when it comes to actual making of a decision on the matter. Therefore, in practical terms, many African Christians live in two worlds of African traditional religion and culture on the one hand

and Christianity on the other. They move easily from one religious practice to the other but not without any qualm. It is therefore important that African Christians are helped out of this dilemma so that they have easiness of mind in the practice of their faith. This was made possible when the Catholic Church, through the Second Vatican Council, clearly promoted inculturation and gave the chance to every people and culture to make the gospel relevant to their local situation and culture.[1] This calls for hard work for African Christian leaders to Africanize the Church and not to take everything verbatim from other continents and use them. This does not do justice to the local Churches in Africa. The present situation in many African Churches tells us that the Church needs to do more in deepening the faith of Christians, and that means rescuing them from what hunts them as Christians responding to their cultural demands. This calls for intensifying the study and education on the subject matter, especially at

---

[1] Read *Evangelii Nuntiandi*, *Redemptories Missio Sacrosanctum Concilium*, in the Second Vatican documents to get a holistic perspective of the Church' s teaching on inculturation. Also, inculturation appeared as one of the five sub-themes of the first Synod of African Bishops and also the deliberations of the 2009 Synod of African Bishops.

the parish and outstation levels. This will be meaningful and successful if the laity themselves are involved in the study and their recommendations taken into account and incorporated in functioning out a liturgy in response to these issues of cultural interest.

I have tried to dilate on two main aspects of African traditional religion and Christianity, namely Childbirth (Naming or outdooring), and Marriage ceremonies. I have already treated the issues of life and death in my book, Christianity and African traditional religion's approach to issues of life and death. In this new book, I have explained the theological understanding of the issues of marriage and childbirth from the perspectives of both African traditional religion and culture and Christianity, and the practical ways by which they are celebrated. I have also given suggestions as to how these two areas of life Cycle of Ghanaian African Christians can be incorporated in the study of inculturating marriage and childbirth, so as give some respite to some Christians who are plunged into this dilemma of how to participate in traditional ritual practices.

I must acknowledge that some of the Catholic parishes in Ghana and Africa are doing their best in addressing these issues but there is the need to deepen and intensify the education of the people in theology and practical ways to deal with these quandaries when they occur. This is what I have tried to do in this little book. If we truly want Ghanaian and African Christians to be true to their calling as Christians, and also to step up our mission of evangelization, then we must work vigorously to make the gospel meaningful to the African way of life. This book is also meant to reach out to non-Christians, especially traditional religious practitioners, to understand and appreciate Christian liturgical celebrations. Such knowledge and understanding would help in peaceful living together of people of various faiths such as African traditional religion and Christianity.

Chapter One

1.0 African Traditional Religion

1.1 Basic Summary of African Traditional Belief System

There are many questions asked about African traditional religion. These questions are reminiscent of those thoughts which were in the minds of the first missionaries when they started their missionary work in Africa, South of the Sahara. Many people, including scholars, ask questions about the original religion of the African people, such as: Do Africans have a religion? Is what they call a religion comparable to any of the world religions like Islam and

Christianity? Is the religion called African traditional religion or African traditional religions? These are interesting questions which some African theologians have tried in their own ways to deal with adequately, but the questions keep on resurfacing which means that more work needs to be done in the study of African traditional religion.

This chapter is not meant to give an in-depth answer to these questions but a general overview of African traditional religion. Let me reiterate what has been pointed out before, that, African traditional religion is part and parcel of the life of the African people. It is for this reason that John Mbiti is said to have made this remarkable statement that Africans are notoriously religious and that all the various ethnic groups have their own religious systems with a set of beliefs and practices.[2] In every ethnic group therefore, one finds out that the people have their belief system, code of ethics, rituals and worship. These are elements which form the foundation of any religion on earth. There is a line, in terms of the belief and practices and code of ethics running through the belief systems of the various

---

[2] Mbiti, J., 1980, African Religions and Philosophy, London, p. 1.

people of Africa. In other words, there are not major differences among the various people and religion in Africa, except of course, language, names, objects used for ritual purposes, artifact and some gestures. For instance, the Akan people of Ghana share with their fellow Africans this fervor for religion but have their own unique ways of going about such traditional beliefs and practices.

I would like to pick on the Akan of Ghana and Ivory Coast, and explore the religion of this people. This would offer us a window into the study of African belief system on matters of marriage and childbirth.

The Akan believe in the One Supreme Being, *Onyankropon,* whom they call *Onyame*,[3] which comes from two Akan words, *nya* meaning "to get" and *me* meaning "to satisfy". So *Nyame* literally means: "the one who satisfies anyone who has him". Kwasi Sarpong intimates that God is considered as the final explanation of all things, rewarding the good and punishing evil.[4] In the Akan Traditional belief God is said to have the ultimate power over life and death. God

---

[3] Sarpong, P. K., 1974, Ghana in Retrospect: Some Aspects of Ghanaian Culture, Tema, p. 9.
[4] Ibid, p. 10.

in the Akan tradition was said to be close to human beings but a mythology explains why He seems to be far away from human being. Peter Sarpong tells of a story of an old woman who despite complaints from God persistently hit God with her pestle and since God could not take it anymore he went higher into the sky. This is to explain the issue of *Deus internos* and *Deus remotes*, which respectively means God near to us and God far away from us. God is spoken of as Almighty, Omnipotent, wholly good, Good Mother (*Obaatampa*), the Creator (*Obooadee*) and many others. God is worshipped through his mediating spirits or gods called *abosom*. He is also the final recipient of libation prayer. This shows that nothing comes after God. He is held in awe and respect.

According to Asare Opoku the ancestors are next to God in the hierarchy of the spiritual beings.[5] They are the departed relations who are in a spiritual state of existence. One needs to fulfill certain criteria to qualify as an ancestor. The first of these criteria is death. For this reason no living person can be described as an ancestor. I should point out that Africans consider death not

---

[5] Opoku, K. A, 1978, West African Traditional Religion, Accra, p. 9.

as an annihilating process but as a way of entering into a new and a different state of life, which is spiritual and a higher form of living than we have here in this life. Those who have died are therefore not really dead but have crossed over to a new spiritual existence and have greater influence on the living here on earth. The death of a person considered as an ancestor should be of a natural cause and not through what the African people describe as bad death, which are for instance: death through suicide, motor accidents, leprosy, childbirth and many others, but death through war qualifies one as an ancestor since the person is fighting in honor for his people. Other qualifications for a person to be an ancestor are: the person should have attained an old age as usually people who die young are not acclaimed as ancestors, except of course the person was a chief or a king. There is the belief that a person who dies young might have died through supernatural causes due to a hidden misdeed committed either by himself or by his family; also, a person is considered for ancestorship should have children since that is a way of helping in the continuity of the lineage. For this reason childless men are disqualified to be ancestors because they are considered in the

African society as children. It is important that the person to be considered as an ancestor was a good person who exhibited good moral aptitude and transparency in his living, conforming to the moral standards and dictates of his society and culture. Misfits in the society are looked down upon and disregarded both when they are alive or dead. For instance, drunks, lazy and irresponsible people, thieves, murderers, criminals, selfish and profligate people do not fit in the qualification of ancestorship. It should be noted that the ancestors are considered as part of the human community, though in the spiritual form, and as such treated with respect, awe and reverence.[6] In fact, they are the custodians of morality.[7] I would like to reiterate here what Peter Sarpong said, that, Africans do not worship ancestors but hold them in high esteem. It is for this reason that many people likened them to the Roman Catholic veneration of the saints.

There are the lesser divinities, called *abosom* in the Akan language. They derive their source of

---

[6] Opoku, K. A, 1978, West African Traditional Religion, Accra, p. 9.
[7] Obeng, P., 1996, "Asante Catholicism", in: Hasting Adrian and Spindler Marc, R, (eds.), Studies of Religion in Africa, Leiden, p. 83.

power from the Supreme Being.[8] The most revealing thing about them is portrayed beautifully by Asare Opoku when he said, "In contrast to God and the ancestors, the lesser deities may be treated with respect or contempt depending on whether they fulfill human aspirations or not."[9] The lesser divinities have their own areas of specialties and are approached depending on their area of competence. The people change to other gods if the one they have is not responding to their needs as they expected. Believers in African traditional religion are not restricted to one god. The gods are taken by people and offered the appropriate rituals depending on their potency. It is therefore up to a particular god to function potently for the adherents otherwise it loses the adherents to other more powerful gods. On the other hand they also expect strict adherence to their regulations otherwise they visit their anger on their worshippers, such as sickness and death.

It is important to state that some families have their own family gods. This may be due to what

---

[8] Opoku, A., 1978, West African Traditional Religion, Accra, p. 9.
[9] Ibid.

these gods might have done in the lives of their ancestors.

There are traditional priests and priestesses who serve the divinities. Many people therefore approach the divinities through these traditional mediators for their needs to be addressed.[10] Their services are highly patronized by people who are looking for riches and fame; barren women who are looking for children; people looking for partners for marriage; business men and women, market men and women who want their businesses to flourish; people looking for visas to travel abroad for greener pastures; and people with all sorts of needs go to the traditional priests or priestesses for these concerns to be addressed. They receive from these priests and priestesses concoctions, amulets or any other objects which are imbued with power to bring into effect the request of the person using them.

There are other spirits, charms, amulets and talisman, *Suman* in the Akan language, used for good and evil purposes. It would not be a surprise to see some Christians with certain talisman tied around their waist for protection

---

[10] Opoku, A., 1978, West African Traditional Religion, Accra, p. 10.

against their enemies and also for their business to prosper. Sometimes these people come to the Church for the talisman to be disposed of because they want to have closer relationship with Jesus Christ. This may also be due to bad conscience or that they are experiencing certain negative tendencies and effects from using this talisman.

The above highlights of the main features of the Akan traditional religion give us a background to the beliefs and practices of the Akan people but also in line with African traditional belief in general. We shall now proceed to look at one of the essential aspects of this study and that is, the Akan concept of marriage.

1.2 The Akan Concept of Marriage

Adulthood for the Akan is a stage of growth and maturity, a time for one to take up the challenges of life with strength, vigor and boldness. Adulthood is a stage when one is said to have attained the age of marriage. One gains independence from the parents and needs a companion for marriage and procreation. There is an Akan proverb which says, *wiase wotra no baanu baanu,*[11] which means that people live in the world in pairs. Another saying about marriage is, "One white ant does not build an anthill". The above sayings are to underscore the importance of the union of two persons in marriage.

Marriage in the Akan traditional sense is when a man and a woman, through traditional rituals are joined together as husband and wife. For the Akans, like their fellow Africans, marriage is so important that it is the focus of existence and it brings together the entire family, which includes the living, the dead and those yet to be born.[12] This comes out clearly in the libation prayer when the ancestors are acknowledged, consulted and their blessings asked for those about to be joined in marriage and upon all those present and petition is asked for fertility and increase in the number of the members. There is an Akan proverb which says *Abusua ye dom,* meaning the family is an army (multitude of people).[13] This is to underline the extended nature of the Akan

---

[11] Opoku, K. A., 1997, Hearing and Keeping, Akan Proverbs, Accra, p. 25.

[12] Mbiti, J. S., 1980, African Religions, and Philosophy, London, p. 133.

[13] Opoku, K. A., 1997, Hearing and Keeping, Akan Proverbs, Accra, p. 28.

family and more so to stress the need for more membership in the family. In the Akan tradition as indicated earlier, the unmarried state is abhorred since it negates the essence of procreation. When people question me about celibacy in the Catholic priesthood and I try to explain to them that priests embrace celibacy to give their lives totally to Jesus Christ and with the grace of God try to live like him in service to God, the Church and the people of God, the immediate remark is, "If we do not marry how do we sustain our society and people? We shall all die and there will be nothing left of us!" These people fail to see the essence of the sacrifice to give up everything for the sake of the gospel. The major concern of these people about marriage is what also underlies Christian marriage namely, procreation and then companionship. In Africa most barren women receive bad treatment from the society, especially the family of the man. When there is barrenness the blame is placed at the doorsteps of the women. They forget that men may also have sterility problems. When there is no issue of a child in marriage, the men are also sometimes ridiculed by the society and this places a challenge on them to prove their capability of fathering children and this is done by finding another woman. But it is important to point out that in general many people are not in favor of concubinage relationship. Concubinage relationship is frowned upon by the traditional Akan society.[14]

The Akan believe that marriage is so important that one should prepare well before going into it. This is buttressed by the proverb which says, *Aware nye nsafufuo na woaka ahwe*, meaning marriage is not palm wine just to be tasted. This is to show that marriage is not a three days journey that you hasten to undertake and when it does not go well then you return. In the same vein, one cannot say he or she is going to marry and when things are not going well then will quit the marriage.[15] Notwithstanding the need to prepare oneself before marriage, any undue delay on the part of the young man to marry will cause his parents or the elders in the lineage to worry and even to interfere in his private life in

---

[14] Sarpong, P. K., 1974, Ghana in Retrospect: Some Aspects of Ghanaian culture, Tema, p. 79

[15] Korang, J, S, N, 1993, "Sankɔfa, Akanfoo Amammemɛ Bi", unpublished thesis submitted to the University College of Education, Winneba, p. 76.

order to advise and encourage him to marry.[16] There may be some freedom in this regards in the cities but this still pertains in the rural areas where the culture is still practiced to a large extent.

There are two types of love, which may drive a person to marriage in the Akan culture. These are *opedo*, which is likeness due to greed for money. It can also be described as romantic love and it is geared towards self-gratification. This type of love does not sustain marriage in the face of problems. The second type of love is the *Odope*, which is true love. One loves not for any selfish motive but for what really a person is. When this type of love forms the basis of a marriage then the marriage becomes a happy and a long lasting relationship.

In Akan marriage one declares his intention to marry to the mother or an elderly person who then in turn informs the father. The father may approve or disapprove of the intention. Then there is the investigation into the family history of the girl. This is in line with the proverb which says, *woko aware bisa*, meaning make enquiries

[16] Gyekye, K., 1996, African Cultural Values: An Introduction, Accra, p. 76.

(ask or investigate) before you marry.[17] This is to say that one does not just go into marriage without preparation, which involves getting to know your partner and the family well in terms of the character and life, hereditary diseases, criminal activities, moral standing, etc of the partner. This is done to avoid disgrace. When the boy's father is satisfied with the investigation the father of the man communicates this information to the girl's parents. The girl's family also does their own investigation and when they are satisfied they also give their approval and consent. They agree on a mutual day for the formal proceeding to commence.

The next step is the *Aponakyibo* or *Aboboamubo* meaning Knocking, which is done by the father of the boy. This constitutes the formal betrothal. It involves provision of drinks (rum or whisky) to the girl's family and a bottle of rum to the girl's father. There is also a token gift to the girl's mother. Gifts are also given to the other women in the mother's family and cash for the girl's brothers and male cousins. We also have to acknowledge the modern trends of betrothal ceremonies whereby additional gifts besides the

---

[17] Opoku, K, A., 1997, Hearing and Keeping, Akan Proverbs, Vol. 2, Accra, p. 26.

customary ones are given. The boy gives gifts like the Bible and ring to the girl. This is a touch of Christian influence on the Akan traditional marriage process.

After this ceremony it is permissible for the two to move together but they are not to engage in sexual activities until the marriage processes are over. The boy is fined if the girl becomes pregnant before the final performance of the customary rites. This fine is called *kwasiabuo sika*.

The next stage of the marriage rites is the giving of the *Tiri aseda*, appreciation fee or *tiri,* head rum. This is the bride wealth and it forms part of the final ceremony, which is performed to bind the couple in a traditional legal wedlock. The bride wealth can be refunded when divorce occurs.

When the date for the coming of the girl is fixed the maternal aunts go for the girl from her house where she is already prepared for her husband. Before they can take the bride away, the woman must give a bottle of schnapps and pay a customary fee, called *akontagye sekan* to the girl's brothers and male cousins. After this, there is merry-making and feasting. There is the marriage meal, *aduane kese*, which is usually prepared by the bride and sent to the groom's house to be enjoyed by him, his relatives and friends.

From the above we see the great involvement of the family in the Akan marriage rituals. It is the family that conducts the marriage even though the consent of the boy and girl is given.

Polygyny, which is the marriage of one man to more than one wife, is accepted and practised among the Akan but due to the influence of Christianity this practice has reduced significantly. Peter Sarpong gives reasons for the practice of polygyny as:

a. First, the issue of considering menstruating women as unclean and therefore cannot cook or do anything for the man;

b. then also the issue of childbirth and the proscription of sexual intercourse for some period;

c. there is also the issue of women outnumbering men in the society and so the excess women should be taken care of to solve the problem of the unmarried woman since an unmarried state is seen as an anomaly and so should be married and taken care of,

d. there is also the issue of economic help, especially on the farm.

e. It is also a sign of prestige to have many wives to produce many children for the family.

f. There is the belief that with many children come the blessing of being remembered after death. The Akan therefore place a high premium on having a large number of descendants.[18]

The Akan culture accepts divorce but does not encourage it. Divorce is the ritual processes by which marriages are dissolved.[19] There are various things to be considered in dissolving a marriage. Some of the reasons are adultery, laziness, barrenness and bad habits like stealing, gossips and not allowing your husband to sleep with you. On the part of the man if he relegates on his duty to look after the wife, gossip about things between him and the wife, continued

---

[18] Cf. Sarpong, P. K., 1974, Ghana in Retrospect: Some Aspects of Ghanaian Culture, Accra, p. 78.
[19] Cf. Korang, J, S, N., 1993, "Sankɔfa, Akanfoɔ Amammemɛ Bi", unpublished thesis submitted to the University College of Education, Winneba, p. 104.

cruelty, magic and witchcraft, desertion, constant state of drunkenness, unforgiving person and lack of personal hygiene. Korang said that some women may not agree to their husbands marrying an additional wife even though he was prepared to compensate her.[20] Some question why one should live in a relationship which is marred by constant tension, pain and suffering and threat of death.

The one who is not happy about the marriage and wants to divorce informs the family head and they look into the case. The family tries to bring the couple together and advise them. If there was no consensus they adjourn the case to another time. There is a saying that *sumiie ma adwene* meaning the pillow gives counsel. If they come again and there is no consent to remain in the marriage the couple come out with what they owe each other and if that is settled, they open a bottle of drink and usually the petitioner pays for the drink. It is also customary for the man to collect the *tiri sika*, head money, which he paid at the beginning of the marriage from the woman. In some of the Akan groups

[20] Cf. Korang, J, S, N., 1993, "Sankɔfa, Akanfoo Amammemɛ Bi", unpublished thesis submitted to the University College of Education, Winneba, p.106.

the marriage is still pending until the family of the woman brings the *tiri sika*. The last act in any Akan divorce case is the *Hyireguo*. The woman goes to the man's house and collects her stuff and the man smears *hyire*, which is white clay, on the feet of the woman as a sign that they are no more and thus she is loosened from her matrimonial bonds.[21] This ritual processes have changed drastically and some of the things written are not done today. What is done today is the family meeting, the opening and pouring of the drink and the presentation of the bride wealth. For instance *hyireguo* even though is part of the divorce process is not done, especially in the cities. I would like to state that divorce is not the original practice of the Akan people. It came as an accident to solve marital problems which are difficult to resolve.

1.3 The Christian Concept of Marriage

The Church defines marriage as a covenant relation between a man and a woman by which they establish between themselves a partnership

---

[21] Cf. Korang, J. S. N., 1993, "Sankɔfa, Akanfoo Amammemɛ Bi", unpublished thesis submitted to the University College of Education, Winneba, p.108.

of their whole life, and which of its own very nature is ordered to the well-being of the spouses and to the procreation and upbringing of children. The Canon of the Church goes further to state that, Christ the Lord has raised marriage between the baptized to the dignity of a sacrament[22] (Can. 1055). [23]

The Church teaches that marriage is a divine institution and this comes out from the creation story in Genesis. When God created man and woman he gave them the injunction to "be fruitful and multiply and fill the earth."(Genesis 1:28). In the Jewish culture the family plays an important role in marriage. The contracting parties are not the bride and groom but the families, that is, the fathers of the spouses. The brothers of the bride had the disposal of the bride if the father were dead (Genesis 24).[24] The bride and the groom had a say in the marriage. They are asked of their opinion and consent as in the case of Rebekah (Genesis 24:57 ff), and sometimes they go against the wishes of their

---

[22] This means that marriage contains grace and confers this grace to those who receive it worthily.

[23] Cf. The Roman Catholic Church, 1983, The Code of Canon Law, London, p. 189.

[24] Cf. McKenzie, J. L, S.J., 1966, Dictionary of the Bible, Ney York, p. 548.

parents as it is evidenced in the case of Samson (Judges 14:2, 5).

The contract between the families was sealed by the payment of the *mōhar*[25] to the parents of the bride (Exodus 22:16).

There is no information on the age at marriage in the Old Testament. McKenzie suggests that it could be not long after puberty.[26]

There was the practice of polygamy and concubinage in the Old Testament but there was clear evidence that monogamy was the one instituted in creation and polygamy was part of the deterioration of humankind which is outlined in Genesis 4. There appears to have been little or no polygamy practiced after the exile. Some of the natural consequences of a polygamous marriage are bickering and envy, sometimes breaking out into hatred and murder.[27]

McKenzie asserts that the highest tribute, which is paid to marriage in the OT, is the adoption of

---

[25] There is a disagreement by scholars on the meaning of the word *Mōhar*. It is generally used to refer to the gift made by the parents to the bride. This is commonly referred to as the dowry. The *Mōhar* could be paid in cash, 50 shekel of silver at the time, (Deuteronomy 22:28 ff) or in service (Genesis 29:18-20).

[26] Cf. McKenzie, J. L, S.J. 1966, Dictionary of the Bible, New York, p. 549.

[27] Cf. Ibid.

the union of marriage as an image of the covenant union and love of Yahweh for Israel (Hosea 2).[28]

The New Testament affirms the indissolubility of marriage and does that by going back to the conception of marriage, Genesis 2:18-25. The Catholic Church, for instance, is against divorce. The Church teaches that the statement in Mark's gospel, "Whoever divorces his wife and marries another commits adultery against her; if she divorces her husband and marries another, she commits adultery" (Mark 10:11-12) correctly represents Jesus' view about divorce. In this quotation Jesus forbade divorce in absolute terms. This is because of Mark's character of frankness and the fact that he does not color whatever he said. The New Testament relates the relationship that exists between the spouses to that between Christ and the Church (Ephesians 5:22-33). The husband and the wife therefore are one body as Christ and the Church are one body.[29]

---

[28] Cf. McKenzie, J. L, S.J. 1966, Dictionary of the Bible, New York, p. 550.
[29] Cf. Ibid. p. 551.

The Church teaches that marriage is a vocation and as such it is a response to the call of Jesus Christ, the Lord.

Jesus also taught on celibacy as a way of life. Celibacy is the practice of abstaining from marriage. The good thing and advantages of celibacy are described by Paul in 1 Corinthians 7:1-38. In the Gospel Jesus exalted celibacy by stating that some people do not marry for the sake of the Kingdom (Matthew 19:10.12). In recent times there have been many problems regarding celibacy and this has led to many questioning its relevant in our modern times. I agree with Archbishop Polycarp Pengo, the Archbishop of Tanzania, when he said that, in matters of priestly celibacy, it is important for everyone concerned to understand the profound religious meaning of the institution in the Church.[30] It is a challenging demand which needs the constant employment and support of the grace of God.

---

[30] Cf. Pengo, P., Priestly Celibacy and Problems of Inculturation, in:
http://www.vatican.va/roman_curia/congregations/cclergy/documents/rc_con_cclergy_doc_01011993_prob_en.html, accessed on the 18.12.2010.

Chapter Two

2.0 African Traditional Religion and childbirth

2.1 The Akan Traditional Concept of Childbirth

Asare Opoku asserts that the birth of a child is the genesis of the life cycle.[31] On the contrary, it should be noted that the beginning of the life cycle could be traced to conception since the African and for that matter the Akan believes that human life begins at conception. Mbiti corroborates this point when he stated in reference to African societies that, "the birth of a child is a process which begins long before the

---

[31] Cf. Opoku, A., 1978, West African Traditional Religion, Juring, Singapore, p.108.

child's arrival in this world and continues long thereafter."[32] The African society recognizes the unborn child. You can argue against this point when you look on the unborn child and even the unnamed child as belonging to the spiritual world as Asare Opoku tries to state, that the Akan call the unnamed child 'ɔhɔho' meaning a visitor.[33] Even though conception is a natural process of procreation, in the Akan traditional belief and thought, it is a divine gift of God. But there are others who say that the gods can be providers of children to barren women. Such children are called *abosom mma* meaning children of the gods. Some people give concrete examples of incidences where the gods have provided children to barren women. The traditional religious practitioners perform the necessary rituals to enable barren women to have children, but they have to dedicate these children to the gods for priestly service and failure to do so have its own fatal consequences.

Childbirth ushers a child into the physical world. The Akan cherish healthy babies and they do not have room for the handicapped. Handicapped

---

[32] Mbiti, J. S., 1969, African Regions and Philosophy, London, p.110.
[33] Cf. Opoku, A., 1978, West African Traditional Religion, Juring, Singapore, p.108

children were considered as a curse to the family and the community. In the olden days such handicapped children were killed. They called them *nsuo mba,* meaning, children of the river. While the practice of killing such people has stopped the thought that they are a curse to the family or community for a wrong thing done in secret or a curse by somebody still lingers on. The same could be said of twins or triplets, who among the Akan were considered as a curse and for that matter, were killed. However, in some of the Akan groups the birth of twins was considered as an extraordinary event and a sign of great fecundity and for this reason they are greeted with, as Mbiti would say, "great joy and satisfaction, as a sign of rich fertility".[34] Mbiti gives an excellent explanation to this when he said that:

"...the birth of twins is something extraordinary, something out of the normal rhythm of things, it gives rise to a feeling of extreme consequences,: either consequences of misfortune, hence the necessity to kill the children (and their mother if need be), or consequences of unusual powers and hence the need to treat such children with

---

[34] Mbiti, J, S., 1980, Africa Religions and Philosophy, London, p. 117.

27

special care or respect. The twins or triplets are not intrinsically evil or extraordinary; it is the unusualness of the event of their birth which makes people attribute extreme association to them."[35]

Children are respected since they could be ancestors who have come back to life. The Akan believe in reincarnation,[36] which is the belief that the dead come back to life through birth into this world again. Those who are reincarnated are both those who are unable to enter the other world since they have to come back to the world to fulfill the conditions[37] necessary for entrance into the world of the spirits and also the ancestors.[38] The belief is that some special features or marks and tattoos on their bodies, are semblances of their departed relatives who were

---

[35] Mbiti, J, S., 1980, Africa Religions and Philosophy, London, p. 117.

[36] Opoku, A., 1978, West African Traditional Religion, Juring, Singapore, p. 108.

[37] The deceased should be an adult even though age is not the only determinant but marital status and position, example a chief; the deceased should have children, should not have died tragically or through diseases like leprosy, dropsy, etc and should not have committed suicide. Peter Sarpong has a lot on the conditions in his book, Ghana in Retrospect, pp.34-35.

[38] Sarpong, P. K., 1974, Ghana in Retrospect: Some Aspects of Ghanaian culture, Tema, p. 39.

prominent in the family. Some family elders are able to identify reincarnated children. They also give special names to such children and treat them with respect and honor, just like the dead relative. An example of such a given name is *Ababio*, which indicates that the person has come back again to life here on earth.

The belief in reincarnation features in the prayers and comments people give during child naming ceremonies.

When a woman experiences the repeated death of her child, certain actions are taken to keep the child alive. This involves the use of talisman on the child, making of signs on the face and body to stop the repeated birth and death and requesting for the assistance of the gods to fortify and protect the child. The child may also be given funny and derogatory names. An example is *Donkor*, which literally means a slave. Some couples who experience the repeated birth and death of a child in their lives have pressure put on them by their families when they go to their hometowns and villages to bath certain herbal preparations given by the traditional priest or priestess and to take some concoctions which are also prepared for them to drink so as to drive away the witches and protect them and the womb of the woman from the destructive powers of witches and sorcerers.

The birth of a child increases the family, clan and society membership. It must be stated that the child is not only for the immediate family, but also for the community and the entire society.

As already stated because barrenness is frown upon whatever should be done to get a child is done if even that person has embraced Christianity. In the past the dead bodies of barren women and men are maltreated so that they do not come back to the earth again in that same situation. I should say that this practice is obsolete and it is not done again. But there is a general disdain for the barren woman. That is why barren women, childless couples, and infertile men earnestly search for the cause and cure of their failure to give birth. They would therefore give or pledge anything short of their lives for a child.[39] Mbiti portrays this situation when he said that, "Unhappy is the woman who fails to get children for whatever qualities she might possess, her failure to bear children is

---

[39] Cf. Appiah-Kubi, K., 1981, Man Cures, God heals, Religion and Medical Practice Among the Akans of Ghana, New York, p. 51.

30

worse than committing genocide: she has become the dead end of human life, not only for the genealogical line but also for herself."[40] Appiah-Kubi summarizes the causes of barrenness in these words, "Barren women sometimes confess to adultery or other sexual offences. Barrenness and Miscarriage are assigned to witchcraft, bad medicine, infidelity, quarrelling or neglecting to propitiate the ancestors and family gods."[41] In many cases barrenness is said to be caused by witchcraft and this is something mostly heard from medicine men and traditional religious practitioners who tell people who go to them that, one or the other member of their families, in many instances the mother or grandmother, who is feeding on the womb or that she has taken the womb away to prevent pregnancy. Rituals are therefore performed to retrieve the womb back to its normal place. But there are exceptional cases of barrenness due to what Fortes describes as premarital laxity on the woman's part and an incompatibility of the different types of 'blood'

---

[40] Mbiti, J. S., 1980, African Religions and Philosophy, London, p. 110.
[41] Appiah-Kubi, K., 1981, Man Cures, God heals, Religion and Medical Practice among the Akans of Ghana, New York, p. 51.

(semen) of the man and the virginal secretion.[42] Some Christians still believe that Traditional religious practitioners and medicine men can provide answers to these crises situations. Hence, some go that far to look for solutions to their problems, since according to them, many fasting, prayers and assurances have not helped them out of their situations and they do not want to remain the laughing stocks of their compatriots.[43]

The genealogical tree is perpetuated through childbirth and it is for this reason that in the Akan society children are precious and cared for by all. The child is for everybody and so everyone is concerned about the growth and maturity of the child. The child is rewarded and punished not only by the immediate parents and family members but the entire community. The traditional family system is stronger in the rural areas but has been somehow affected by modernism and urbanization in the cities. In the Urban centres the concentration is tilting

---

[42] Cf. Fortes, M., 1954, 'A Demographic Field Study in Ashanti, in: Lorimer, F., (ed.), *Culture and Human Fertility*, U.N.E.S.C.O, p. 266.

[43] Peter Sarpong has a lot of information on this subject in his book, Girls' Nubility Rites in Ashanti, Accra, 1991, pp.7-9.

towards the nucleus family than the external family system, which is the practice of the African people, including the Akan. In the external family system, the care of children is not left in the hands of only the parents but the entire family of uncles, aunts, cousins and nieces. This breakdown of the external family system is one of the contributing factors to the presence of many children we have on our streets today in the urban centres.

In the Akan traditional thought the spouses are supposed to be faithful to each other. The failure of one or the other to be true and faithful may lead to certain complications during childbirth, including difficult delivery and death of the child or the mother or even miscarriage. Kofi Appiah-Kubi has stated that children do not normally survive in quarrelsome or adulterous homes and that safe deliveries in such situations are very rare.[44] There is the need for elaborate rituals for the purposes of purification or reparation.

---

[44] Cf. Appiah-Kubi, K., 1981, Man Cures, God Heals, Religion and Medical Practice among the Akans of Ghana, New York, p. 55.

Also, it is a taboo[45] for a husband and the wife, who is pregnant, to have sex in the farm. This is because the farm is the abode of the gods and such an act defiles the land. This may bring about infertility of the land leading to famine. It may also bring about difficulty in childbirth. Here too, elaborate rituals are needed to appease the gods. But the real rational behind this may be the dangers that these couple may face having sex in the forest. They are exposed to dangerous animals, poisonous reptiles and insects which may pose a danger to their lives.

It must be pointed out that abortion was frowned upon and has no place in the Akan traditional practices. In the traditional society young people engage in sexual relationship within the context of marriage, when they are adults. That is why they had the puberty rites to usher young girls into womanhood. Anyone who got pregnant before the puberty rites was punished severely. Peter Sarpong brings out the seriousness of the issue when he said that:

"A girl who indulged in sexual adventure prior to her initiation was severely punished,

---

[45] Taboos are prohibitions of an ethnic group or a community, which should be followed so as not to bring punishment on oneself or the society.

sometimes with death, particularly if she had not reached physiological puberty. If, on the other hand, it was found out that she was biologically mature but had still to be socially declared so through the performance of the rites, then she was ritually cleansed and purified, and then punished with a fine or something less stringent than would have been meted out to her if she had been below the age of physiological puberty".[46]

This was probably to check teenage pregnancy and abortion. It was also because the traditional family abhors illegitimate children. Children should come from a proper marital relationship. Pre-marital sex was really checked so that there would not be the occasion for people to abort their babies and probably kill an ancestor since this may cause the anger of the ancestors and bring misfortune not only to the individual but the entire family and community.

The traditional society saw to it that marriages are correctly contracted so that the couples could have the freedom to live together and procreate. Since pregnancy is a clear sign that a child is going to be born and incorporated into the society, the expectant mother becomes a special

---

[46] Sarpong, P. K., 1974, Ghana in Retrospect: Some Aspects of Ghanaian Culture, Accra-Tema, p. 74.

person and therefore receives special attention and treatment.

From the foregoing, I would say that, because of the premium that is put on childbirth that women would do everything possible to look for a child, including seeking for spiritual assistance from one or the other deity, and also seeing children as a probable ancestor, the child born is given all the love and protection both materially and spiritual to grow to be strong and useful to the society.

Right from the moment of conception, the joy and happiness of a new human being is celebrated with joy and this also calls for the parents to observe strict ethical discipline to ensure the safe arrival of the child.

The traditional Akan did not use contraceptives as we know it today. There was a strict discipline for the man to keep away from wife right after childbirth until after a certain period of time. That was also the reason for polygamy in the Akan traditional society.

Children born into this life have their own destiny, which they brought to this world, either given to them directly by the Supreme Being or at their own request sealed by the Supreme

Being.[47] Many actions and inaction, and also successes and failures of the Akan are attributed to destiny. This is called in Akan, *hyebia* or nkrabea. We must acknowledge the observation of Peter Sarpong that, "This of course does not imply that the African does not believe in personal responsibility. It is only the inexplicable habitual traits of a person, either towards good or evil, which are explained through appeal to destiny."[48] That is why people are held accountable for their action and it is not excused on their destiny.

2.2. The Names and Rites of Naming in Akan Traditional Religion

Korang defines name as an identification that is given to human beings and things so as to know their differences.[49] This shows that everyone is unique. There is an Akan proverb which says, *asisie nti na yekyee din* meaning, it is because of

---

[47] Cf. Opoku, A., 1978, West African Traditional Religion, Accra, p. 100.

[48] Sarpong, P. K., 1974, Ghana in Retrospect: Some Aspects of Ghanaian Culture, Accra-Tema, p. 38.

[49] Cf. Korang, J, S, N, 1993, Sankɔfa, Akanfoɔ Amammemɛ Bi, unpublished thesis submitted to the University College of Education, Winneba, p. 59.

cheating that everyone was given a name.[50] This touches on the responsibility of the individual. One has to bear the responsibility of his or her actions or inactions. The Akans, like their fellow Africans, place much importance on names. The name of everyone is so important since there is an identity between the name and the person who bears that name, and this name can bring blessings or a curse.[51] The Akan therefore do not just give names to their children. They take into consideration so many factors which are the day that a person was born, the experiences of a person like miscarriage, the way and manner of birth of a person like a child who is said to be given to the parents by the gods.[52] The names that are given to a person may be based on the day that a person is born. The Akan believe in seven deities, who represent the seven days of the week, and according to the day of the week that a person is born on, that person is supposed to inherit the personality of the corresponding

---

[50] Cf. Korang, J, S, N, 1993, Sankɔfa, Akanfɔo Amammemε Bi, unpublished thesis submitted to the University College of Education, Winneba, p.59.
[51] Cf. Ibid. p. 88.
[52] Cf. Ibid. p. 59.

deity.[53] We represent below a diagram on this issue of the deity and names and the significance of the names as represented by Nkansa-Kyeremanteng:

Diagram.[54]

DAY		DEITY	DEITY
ENGLISH	TWI	ENGLISH	TWI
Sunday	Kwasi-da	Sun	Ayisi(Awi-sa)
Monday	Dwow-da	Moon	Adwo
Tuesday	Benada	Tiu	Bena
Wednes-day	Wuku-da	Woden (Odin)	Wuku
Thurs-day	Yawda	Thor	Yaw
Friday	Fida	Frigg(Frig-ga)	Afi
Saturday	Memen-da	Saturn	Ame

---

[53] Cf. Rutledge, C. K., "African Traditional Religious Beliefs, among the Akans", in: http://colanmc.siu.edu/BAS495/students/chris/ghweb.html , accessed on the 17.12.2010.
[54] Nkansa-Kyeremateng, K, 1999, Akan Heritage, Accra, p.141.

These are the day names of almost every Akan. It is the soul name or *kradin*[55]. Then we have the by-name, which is attached to the day name. Kwasi Sarpong gives an example as *Kwadwo* or *Adowa Akota* for a Monday child.[56] Sometimes when there is more than one person born on a particular day in a family they add either *panyin*, meaning elder, and an example is Kwame Panyin; or *ketiwa*, small, or Kwame kitiwa. The child is also given a proper name which may be the name of the father, an uncle, a brother, a friend, a sister, either dead or alive, as gratitude and honor for the person, and the prayer is that the child will grow to be like the person after whom he is named.[57] One may also take the name of one's father but this is not automatic.[58] Names of deities are also given as gratitude to the deity for an answered prayer for a child. Peter Sarpong makes mention of names like *Amisa* and *Tanɔ* which are names of some rivers in Ghana. Names are also given based on the

---

[55] This is supposed to be the day that a person bid farewell from the creator to come to this world of the living. So the day of birth is the day of farewell from the unseen world and also arrival to this world.

[56] Sarpong, P. K., 1974, Ghana in Retrospect: Some Aspects of Ghanaian Culture, Accra-Tema, p. 88.

[57] Ibid. p. 89.

[58] Cf. Ibid. p. 88.

circumstances of the birth of the child. An example is *Adiyaa,* which means, has suffered, and those born on certain feast days like *Adae, fofie,* and so on, are given such names also. Sarpong also talks about funny names given to children to prevent repeated death of a child so that it will stay. An example is *Asaseasa* meaning, there is No-More-Ground.[59]

From the foregoing it is clear that the Akan may have many names and the relatives and friends may use these names for him or her. It is important to note that when one becomes a chief one changes the name and takes on a stool name. An example is the King of Ashante who was known in public life as Barima Kwaku Dua but as a King he is now called Nana Osei Tutu II.

The above exposition shows that names are very important and when one is not given a name in the Akan society it means that the person does not belong to the society as yet. This may explain why when a woman experiences repeated death of her children, at a point the child is not named until the society is sure that it has come to stay.[60]

---

[59] Cf. Sarpong, P. K., 1974, Ghana in Retrospect: Some Aspects of Ghanaian Culture, Accra-Tema, p. 90.
[60] Cf. Ibid.

Since a child who died before the naming ceremony, which is traditionally done on the eighth day, is not seen as part of the society as yet, there was no wailing and the parents were compelled to put on white dress as a sign of happiness. The dead child is disposed of in a dishonorable way, like being thrown into an incinerator.[61] This was to let the child feel ashamed of the treatment and not to return to repeat that painful situation again. There is the belief that with this kind of treatment, when the child comes again, it would come to stay. We have to acknowledge that this practice has died out in the cities and even in the villages. This may be due to the advent of new insights into causes of death due science.

The naming ceremony for the Akan, as already described, is on the eighth day. Korang explains why this ceremony is performed on the eight day when he said that, the Akan have a belief that there is a spiritual and unseen world beyond this existence and in this unseen world there are parents for every human being, and for that reason if a child is born and it is able to live for eight days then it means that the parents in the

---

[61] Cf. Sarpong, P. K., 1974, Ghana in Retrospect: Some Aspects of Ghanaian Culture, Accra-Tema, p. 90.

unseen world have permitted it to come and live among the living here on earth. The earthly parents then clear all the old clothing that have been used for the whole period before the eighth day and put them into the refuse dump as a sign that the child has parted company with the parents in the unseen world. Among the Akans therefore it is not permissible for a child less than the eighth day to see the sun or to come outside of the room.[62] The rites of naming are ceremonies that are performed to show that the child has been accepted as a member of the human race. If the child is accepted then there should be a mark on the child to indicate its existence among the living and that mark is the name that is given to it.[63]

Peter Sarpong said that it is the father of the child who appoints the day for the naming ceremony, which is usually the day on which he was born.[64] On the eighth day, the child is brought outside and the ceremony performed for it to incorporate it into the human community.

---

[62] Cf. Korang, J. S. N, 1993, Sankɔfa, Akanfoɔ Amammemɛ Bi", unpublished thesis submitted to the University College of Education, Winneba, p. 71.
[63] Cf. Ibid. p. 70.
[64] Cf. Sarpong, P. K., 1974, Ghana in Retrospect: Some Aspects of Ghanaian Culture, Accra-Tema, p. 91.

The child is well prepared by the maternal grandmother and *hyire* put on the child. *Hyire* is a white substance symbolizing a sign of victory. The child is then sent to the father's house for the naming, and a representative of the father performs this, and according to Peter Sarpong it is usually the sister.[65] In Accra, people call on any distinguished person in the community whom they know to do the naming. The reason given is that their family elders are not readily available and it is also much more expensive to bring them from their hometowns and villages to come and perform the ceremony. The other issue too is that some postpone the naming ceremony to a convenient day and not necessarily on the eighth day.

Another social change creeping into the traditional naming ceremony is that in some cases they are advertised in newspapers and on radio stations and a whole lot of people are invited to come for the ceremony. Afterwards, they have music and dancing. I should remark that in the urban centres naming ceremonies

---

[65] Cf. Sarpong, P. K., 1974, Ghana in Retrospect: Some Aspects of Ghanaian Culture, Accra-Tema, p. 91.

have become 'a show business'[66] and also people are doing it with the intention of getting money from those invited for the occasion. In other words, naming ceremonies have become a business venture. In spite of this what is essential in the ceremonies are performed.

The child is brought outside and laid on a mat and the one who is to perform the rites names the child and puts water into the mouth and tells the child that when it is water it should say so and then he does the same with the wine and tells the child that when it is wine it should say so. This is an education in truth, honesty and integrity, which are cherished by the traditional society.

During the ceremony of out-dooring libations are poured to ask for the guidance of God, the gods and the ancestors for the child. The prayers ask for a good character, hardwork, fruitfulness, truthfulness, justice and protection for the child. These are virtues expected of every member of the traditional family and the hope is that the child will grow up exhibiting these qualities and would become a good ambassador of the

---

[66] By this they mean that people do the naming ceremony in an extravagant manner and in this way it loses some of its traditional significance and touch.

parents, the family and the entire society wherever it finds itself in the future.

Chapter Three

3.0 Childbearing in Christianity

3.1 Roman Catholic Church's Belief and Teaching on Childbearing

In the Old Testament the first blessing uttered upon human beings in the creation story was that human beings are to be fruitful and multiply, and to fill the earth (Genesis 1:28). It is for this reason that a large family was a blessing from God (Psalms 127:3-5; 128:2-4). For the Jews childlessness was seen as a curse and a great sorrow (Genesis 30:1; Is 4:1; Luke 1:25). There is an emphasis on quality of children rather than quantity and this means that there is therefore no desire for a multitude of unprofitable children.[67]

---

[67] Cf. McKenzie, J. L., S. J., 1996, Dictionary of the Bible, New York, p. 129.

The Jews desired sons more than daughters and it is usually the firstborn son who succeeded to the authority of the father.[68]

Jesus as a child was obedient to his parents (Luke 2:51) and he settled the dispute among his disciples about priority by placing a child before them and insisting that they must become like children (Matthew 18:1), that means they must become the least important of all.[69]

The Church teaches that parents must regard their children as *"children of God* and respect them as *human persons"*[70] Parents have the responsibility for the education of their children and this can be done when they create a home where there is tenderness, forgiveness, respect fidelity and disinterested service as the rule. The home should also be a place for the education in the virtues for the children.[71]

It is because of the value that the Church places on childbearing, which is a gift of God, that, it is against anything that is against life. I would like

---

[68] McKenzie, J. L., S. J., 1996, Dictionary of the Bible, New York, p. 129.

[69] Ibid. p. 130.

[70] The Roman Catholic Church, 1994, Catechism of The Catholic Church, London, p. 480.

[71] Cf. Ibid.

to mention some of these issues according to the position of the Catholic Church.

The Catholic Church therefore is against intentional murder: "The deliberate murder of an innocent person is gravely contrary to the dignity of the human being, to the golden rule and to the holiness of the Creator. The law forbidding it is universally valid: it obliges each and everyone, always and everywhere."[72]

The Catholic Church is against abortion. The Church teaches that direct abortion, which is abortion willed either as an end or a means, is gravely contrary to moral law. It is in this vein that the Church teaches that human life must be respected and protected absolutely from the moment of conception: "From the very first moment of his existence, a human being must be recognized as having the rights of a person- among which is the inviolable right of every innocent being to life"[73] The Catholic Church's respect for human life is seen in the penalty which is attached to committing such a crime,

---

[72] The Roman Catholic Church, 1994, Catechism of The Catholic Church, London, p. 480.
[73] Ibid. p. 489.

which is the canonical penalty of excommuni-cation[74] (Canons 1398 and 1314).

The Catholic Church is also against euthanasia, which is referred to as 'Mercy Killing'. The stand of the Church is that whatever the motives and means, direct euthanasia consists in putting an end to the lives of handicapped, sick or dying persons. The Church's stand is that it is morally unacceptable. Those whose lives are diminished or weakened deserve special respect. Those who are sick or handicapped should be assisted to lead lives as normal as possible. This aspect of the Church's teaching is significant in the light of what happened to deformed children in the traditional society in the past. Today some handicapped children are hidden from the public view because some people think it is a disgrace to the dignity of their persons and families. This has raised concerns in public circles and institutions are springing up to cater for the needs of such people.

The Catholic Church is also against suicide. The Church teaches that it is God alone who is the sovereign Master of life. Human beings are stewards and it is God who has entrusted our

---

[74] This means that one is banned totally from having any communion or anything to do with the Catholic Church.

lives unto human being and so therefore human beings are to be responsible for their lives before God and preserve them for God's honor their the salvation of their souls.

The Church teaches all to uphold life and live a worthy and moral life. Human beings are to be concerned about the integral well-being of all peoples. They must see to it that there is food and clothing, housing, healthcare, basic education, employment and social assistance for all peoples.

The Church is concerned about the human person from conception to death and even beyond. The Catholic Church has prayers for pregnant women and the child in the womb. For instance,

"Lord God,
Creator of the human race,
Your Son, through the working of the Holy Spirit, was born of a woman,
So that he might pay the age-old debt of sin
And save us by his redemption.

Receive with kindness the prayer of your servant
As she asks for the birth of a healthy child.

Grant that she may safely deliver a son or a Daughter to be numbered among your family,
To serve you in all things, and to gain eternal life.
We ask this through Christ our Lord.
R: Amen.[75]

Children are also baptized as infants in response to Jesus Christ asking the little ones to come to him. We are not going into the reasons for infant baptism but it is important to say that this has been the practice of the Church since its inception.

3.2 The Rites of Naming in the Roman Catholic Church

Among the Jews names were considered to be more than an artificial tag which distinguishes one person from another. The name of a person has a mysterious identity with him or her and can thus be considered as a substitute for the person, as acting or receiving in his or her

---

[75] The Roman Catholic Church, 1990, Shorter Book of Blessings, New York, p. 105

place.[76] Every name given to a person has a meaning and for that matter the name does not only distinguish the person but also tells one the kind of person someone is. There is a belief among the Jews that the knowledge of the name of a person gives control and the utterance of the name is effective either upon its bearer or as containing the power of the person whose name is uttered.[77]

In the Old Testament personal names were significant as it expresses certain religious beliefs or a prayer of petition. A person's name gives fame and reputation and also survives in his descendants. It is therefore a disaster when someone's name is destroyed or blotted out (I Samuel 24:21; 2Kgs 14:27).[78]

Among the Jews a change in the personal name indicated a change in the person and a typical example is the change of the name of Abram to Abraham (Genesis 17:5).[79] In the OT to know the name of Yahweh is to experience the reality which the name signifies, which is the reality of assured confidence and deliverance (Psalm 9:16;

---

[76] McKenzie, J. L., S.J., 1996, Dictionary of the Bible, New York, p. 603.
[77] Ibid.
[78] Ibid.
[79] Ibid.

Isaiah 52:6). The name of Yahweh is also his reputation and his glory (Exodus 9:16)[80].

McKenzie states that in the New Testament, the most remarkable development on the concept of name is the way the theology of name is applied to Jesus and this is said to be a testimonial of the divinity of Jesus himself.[81] Jesus' disciples invoked his name and this empowered them to work many miracles (Mark 16:17). Also, through faith in the name of Jesus Christians are to obtain eternal life (John 3:18: 1Jn 5:13).

McKenzie gives a description of naming of Jewish children by saying that among the Jews when a child is born the news was announced to the father who presumably was not present (Job 3:3). The new infant was bathed, rubbed with salt, wrapped in bands (Ezekiel 16:4); Luke 2:7). Circumcision was done on the 8th day after birth (Leviticus 12:3; Luke 1:59; 2:21). In ancient times it was the responsibility of the father to circumcise the child (Genesis 17:23; 21:4). The newborn baby was received on the knees of the father, who thus acknowledge the child (Job 3:12), perhaps by a formula such as that of

---

[80] McKenzie, J. L., S.J., 1996, Dictionary of the Bible, Great Britain, p.604.
[81] Ibid.

Psalm 2:7. When a slave is substituted for the wife, the child was delivered upon the knees of the wife (Genesis 30:3). The name was conferred either by the father (Genesis 4:26; 5:3, 29) or by the mother (Genesis 4:1, 25; 29:23) but neighbors (Ruth 4:17) and relatives (Luke 1:59) could influence the choice of name. In the OT account the name was given at birth, however, in the NT it is given at the time of circumcision (Luke 1:59ff; 2:21) and it was a rule that mothers should nurse their children for a period of two to three years (Genesis 21:7).[82]

The education and rearing of children was entirely in the hands of the parents as it was their obligation to teach their children wisdom. This was especially necessary before the time of the synagogue which begun the period of the education of Jewish children.[83]

The Church acknowledges the importance of names to the individual and also the human community. A person becomes a member of the Church through baptism. Baptism is the means by which people become Christians and as such

---

[82] McKenzie, J. L., S.J., 1996, Dictionary of the Bible, New York, p.129.
[83] Ibid.

"Other Christ".[84] For the Church it is the time of naming for the Child and so the celebrant who is cleric asks the parent "What name do you give to your child?" or "What name have you given to your child?"[85] It is important to note that someone other than the parents may give the reply to this question if the local custom gives him the right to name the child.[86] A scripture text is read and the child is then baptized with water. This water is usually poured on the forehead three times whilst mentioning the name of the child. During the ceremony of baptism the child is also signed with the oil of Chrism to make it a partaker in the priesthood, prophet-hood, and kingship of Jesus Christ. The oil of the Catechumens is to drive away evil spirits and dedicate the child to God. Whiles the oils are being administered prayers are said for the child. White garment is also placed on the child as an outward sign of its Christian dignity and an injunction on the child to live a good Christian life. A lighted candle is given to the parents for the child to signify that the child is enlightened by Christ and thus encouraged to keep its faith

---

[84] The Roman Catholic Church, 1970, The Rites of Baptism, Minnesota, p. 1.
[85] Ibid. p. 3.
[86] Ibid. p. 1

alive and go out to meet Christ when he comes again. Prayers are said over the ears and the mouth to enable the child to hear the Word of God and the mouth to proclaim the faith to the praise and glory of God the Father.[87] There is a reading from the Bible and then reflections on the reading. Parents and Godparents or sponsors are to reject sin and profess faith in Christ Jesus on behalf of the children about to be baptized. The Church encourages her faithful to take the names of saints to serve as role model for their lives. In Africa some people like to take their own African names. Prayers and blessings are said for the child, the parents and all who are present to witness to the occasion.

---

[87] The Roman Catholic Church, 1970, The Rites of Baptism, Minnesota, p. 12.

Chapter Four

4.0 Inculturating African Traditional Marriage

4.1 Practical Ways

During the early days of missionary activities in Africa, it was the ardent preoccupation and desire of the missionaries to Christianize Africans and save their souls. This was because they wrongly thought that the souls of Africans were dammed to everlasting fire. In this endeavor, everything African was seen as contrary to Christian belief. The missionaries mistakenly construed western way of life as representing Christianity and as such Africans had to abandon their cherished cultural practices in favor of the western Christian culture. They therefore condemned and prohibited almost all African cultural practices and a typical example was what has to do with African marriage. For instance, polygyny, bridewealth, and even singing and dancing during these ceremonies were outlawed. They believed in their own form of marriage ritual which was composed based on their cultural practices otherwise they would have followed Jewish marriage practices. They could not adjust to the African way of doing their own thing and try to understand it and inculturate this culture into Christianity. This is exactly what is happening in many African Churches today. They take the western liturgy and implant that whole and entire in the African context.

It is my conviction that the Christian elements in terms of matter and form cannot be done away with but what we need to Africanize should be done to make the celebrations relevant to the African people. It is in this direction that I would like to suggest that the traditional marriage celebration should be merged to that of the Christian one, and this means that, what is good in the tradition should be baptized and inculturated into Christianity to ensure judicious use of time and make the celebration cost effective. As at now many African Christians try to inculturate some Christian elements in the traditional marriage ceremonies. This is something that Vatican II supports since such an inculturation assist in the mission of the Church to evangelize. This becomes necessary also as one hears of the huge debt that people incur after a marriage ceremony. Both the traditional and Christian marriage ceremonies cost a lot of money but since marriage means a lot to the people some of them invest all they have on it and thereafter live in hardship and poverty.

The conclusion of the traditional marriage celebration is wrongly viewed by many people as the engagement ceremony for the Christian rite. In actual fact when the traditional marriage is sealed the man and the woman traditionally become husband and wife.

The Christian Church demands that they come again to the Church for another wedding. Interestingly, the priest goes to the final traditional celebration and blesses the ring and the bible to signify a Christian marriage engagement. This is unnecessary a duplicity, superfluous and waste of money and time.

Since the Church demands that traditional marriage celebration is a prerequisite for Church celebration it is a sign of recognition of the tradition of the people. The suggestion I want to make is that, Christian marriage should be fixed on the final day of the traditional marriage celebration so that the priest is in attendance and with the other required witnesses to solemnize the marriage and issue the necessary certified documents. This final rite could take place on the same day in the Church so that the marriage vows are exchanged and the marriage Christianized. This may satisfy the law that the place of marriage should be gazetted.

4.2 Practical Ways of Inculturating the Ghanaian Traditional Naming Ceremony

Naming ceremony is an important element in African culture. It ushers a child into the world and so most parents celebrate it so that the child will have the protection of God, the spirits and ancestors. In most cases the parents ask for a Christian naming ceremony because they do not want the use of any alcoholic beverage for the child. Also, they do not want the pouring of libation by which the names of the spirits are mentioned. They want to place the Child in the hands and care of Jesus Christ. In short, they

62

want to Christianize the traditional celebration of out-dooring or naming ceremony. Some of the Catholic dioceses in Ghana, for instance the Ho Catholic diocese has inculturated the traditional rites of naming into the Christian Infant baptismal ritual. The symbols employed in the traditional rites could be adopted for use by the celebrant. Discussing the issue of inculturating the traditional ritual of naming ceremony among the Ewe people of Ghana, Michael Okyerefo enumerates some of the symbols which are shared between the Ghanaian culture and that of Christianity in terms of infant baptism as darkness and light or sin and goodness and went on to say that, "Where baptism is performed, the water that is used as a symbol of cleansing and new life in the Christian rite reinforces the traditional virtue of honesty required by traditional culture."[88]

A substance like *hyire* which is smeared on the child as a sign of victory has nothing unchristian about it and could still be maintained. The elements like water, alcoholic drink or salt

---

[88] Okyerefo, M. P. K., March 23-25, 2009, "Spirituality and Historic Mission Christianity in Africa: Ghanaization in Roman Catholicism", in: African Christian Spirituality and Mission' – Akrofi-Christaller Memorial Institute, Akropong-Akwapim, p. 8.

which are dropped on the tongue of the child is symbolic. Therefore it is not a problem to substitute them with non-alcoholic drink. The symbolism of the elements used in the traditional naming ceremonies touch on the world of the people into which the child is born. The same applies in the Christian tradition where water is used to usher the child into the life, death and resurrection of Jesus Christ; the oil of catechumens which is to signify the driving away of darkness, evil and Satan from the child; the oil of Chrism which is to unite the child to Jesus Christ in his threefold function of priest, prophet and king. Other elements like the candle lit from the Easter candle symbolizing Christ and admonition to the child to live in the light of Christ and the signing of the cross on the lips and the ears of the child is to commission it to proclaim the gospel and listen to the word of God. Both the Ghanaian traditional naming ceremony and the Christian Infant baptism are full of symbols and the proper study of the two by a liturgical commission and merging them for Christians would be welcome news for Ghanaian Christians. This will solve the issue of duplicity of things as regards traditional naming ceremony and Christian baptism.

Conclusion

From the discussions so far one could say that in spite of the challenges inherent in marriage life, Ghanaians and for that matter Africans cherish it and every support is given to people who want to marry. In fact, as stated already not to marry is a shame and the society looks down on such a person, except of course for religious reasons. This was the initial problem with Catholic celibacy and chastity for priests and religious. The perpetuation of the lineage is what drives such attitude to marriage. It is for this reason that the society taunts the unmarried to encourage people to go into it. I underlined the fact that many people have embraced the Christian faith and for this reason, it is important to merge the traditional marriage ritual with that of the Church so that we avoid duplicity and senseless waste of time and money.

The same applies to the Ghanaian naming ceremony and the rites of Infant Baptism. Some dioceses in Ghana have begun such a process of inculturation. It is important for the leaders of the Church to set up committees or the commissions responsible for research into such issues take up the challenge and fashion out something concrete for the Bishops' Conference to dilate on and if permission is needed from the Vatican they ask for it for a uniform inculturated celebration of marriage and naming ceremony in Ghana.

I am sure that these are not big issues that cannot be done. We have the experts and the necessary encouragements should be given to them to work on these issues that affect the people in their faith expression so as to help both the priests and the laity. That is what the Second Vatican document is promoting, that the gospel is made relevant to the culture of the people and that is an ongoing study and effort.

Bibliography

Appiah-Kubi, K., 1981, Man Cures, God heals, Religion and Medical Practice among the Akans of Ghana, New York.

Fortes, M., 1954, 'A Demographic Field Study in Ashanti', in: Lorimer, F., (ed.) *Culture and Human Fertility*, U.N.E.S.C.O.

Gyekye, K., 1996, African Cultural Values, An Introduction, Accra,

Korang, J, S, N., 1993, "Sankɔfa, Akanfɔo Amammemɛ Bi", unpublished thesis submitted to the University College of Education, Winneba.

Mbiti, J, S, 1980, Africa Religions and Philosophy, London.

McKenzie,J. L, S.J., 1966, Dictionary of the Bible, Great Britain.

Nkansa-Kyeremateng, K, 1999, Akan Heritage, Accra.

Obeng, P., 1996, "Asante Catholicism" in Hasting, A., and Spindler Marc, R., (eds.), Studies of Religion in Africa, Leiden.

Okyerefo, M. P. K., March 23-25, 2009, "Spirituality and Historic Mission Christianity in Africa: Ghanaization in Roman Catholicism", in: African Christian Spirituality and Mission' – Akrofi-Christaller Memorial Institute, Akropong-Akwapim.

Opoku, A., 1978, West African Traditional Religion, Juring, Singapore.

Opoku, K, A, 1997, Hearing and Keeping, Akan Proverbs, Vol.2, Accra.

Sarpong, P. K., 1974, Ghana in Retrospect: Some Aspects of Ghanaian Culture, Tema.

Sarpong, P. K., Girls' Nubility Rites in Ashanti.

The Roman Catholic Church, 1970, The Rites of Baptism, Minnesota.

The Roman Catholic Church, 1994, Catechism of the Catholic Church, London.

The Roman Catholic Church, 1983, The Code of
Canon Law, London.

Internet Source

Pengo, P., Priestly Celibacy and Problems of
Inculturation, in:
http://www.vatican.va/roman_curia/cong
regations/cclergy/documents/rc_con_ccle
rgy_doc_01011993_prob_en.html,
accessed on the 18.12.2010.

Other Books by the Author:

Rev. Fr. Dr. Eric Kwabena Oduro Wiafe

Title: **Inter-religious Dialogue and Cooperation among the three Major Religions of Ghana**

Project Summary:

In Africa, there is a growing awareness, even among scholars, that there have not been much constructive dialogue between Christianity,

African traditional Religion (ATR) and Islam. But such Inter-religious dialogue is necessary for peace in the world as religion holds a major place in fostering social integration, mutual understanding and peaceful convivance. Religion also serves as a catalyst for world peace. The study examines the case of Inter-religious dialogue in Ghana and the efforts being made to encourage adherents of the different religious groups to engage in Inter-religious dialogue and Cooperation as a way of demolishing the walls of prejudice stone by stone and build bridges of dialogue rather than erect barriers of hatred, vengeance and hostility (Cf.. Hans Küng, 2007). Ghana is a democratic and relatively stable and peaceful country, but there have been cases of religiously motivated violence and so in order to bring peace and understanding there is the necessity for Inter-religious dialogue.

Religion influences the daily lives and activities of the people in Ghana in a significant way. Therefore, the study looks at two major belief systems and practices in Ghana, namely, witchcraft, which has led to the establishment of the witchcraft colony in Gambaga among others, and the belief and practice of Trokosi, which is a practice whereby a family gives out a girl-child to the traditional shrine to serve there for a period of time as a reparation due to an offence committed by a member of her family. We examined how through Inter-religious dialogue such beliefs and practices could be handled and consensus built up for peaceful living together. This is based on the truism that, in a society, where there exist various religious groups, like in the case of Ghana, constructive dialogue can help the people find solutions to major challenges confronting them, which otherwise may lead to violence and instability. In this study therefore, the necessity of inter-religious dialogue for Ghana becomes a Sine qua non to explore ways and means to overcome prejudice, to live and work together for peace and progress in Ghana.

Language: English
Year of Publication: 2010
Number of pages: 190
ISBN: 978-3-86624-498-6
PREMIUM
Publisher: dissertation.de - Verlag im Internet GmbH
Book Price: 43.50 EUR

PDF-Price: 25.88 EUR

Book found in:

    a. http://www.amazon.de/Inter-religious-
        dialogue-among-three-
        religions/dp/3866244983/ref=sr_1_1?ie=
        UTF8&s=books-intl-
        de&qid=1291759824&sr=8-1
    b. http://www.dissertation.de/buch.php3?bu
        ch=6120

**Title: The three major Religions in Ghana:
History, Theology and Influence**

73

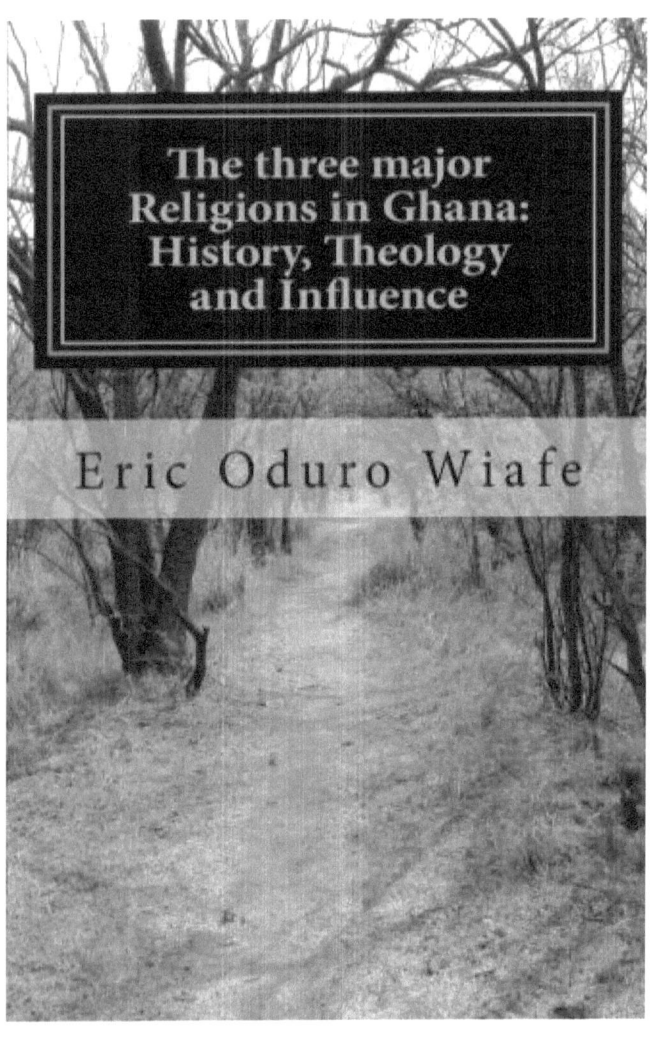

The three major
Religions in Ghana:
History, Theology
and Influence

Eric Oduro Wiafe

Project Summary:

African Traditional Religion, Christianity and Islam are the three major religious groups in Ghana. They play a prominent and significant role in the holistic life of Ghanaians from the political, economical, educational, religious and the family. This experience is not only limited to Ghana but the entire African continent.

The purpose of this book is to help people not only to know about their religious faith but also the religious faith of their neighbors so that they can live in mutual respect, peace and convivance.

List Price: $29.99
6" x 9"   (15.24 x 22.86 cm)
Number of pages: 176
ISBN-13: 978-1456350581
ISBN-10: 1456350587

Book Found in:

    a. https://www.createspace.com/3498839
    b. http://www.amazon.de/s/ref=nb_sb_noss ?__mk_de_DE=%C5M%C5Z%D5%D1

&url=search-alias%3Daps&field-keywords=eric+wiafe&x=0&y=0

Title: The Role of Religion in Poverty Alleviation in Africa

Project Summary:

Is Africa a poor continent, a continent without hope? The answer is straightforward and definitely NO. Africa is not poor. The people are also not poor but they have been made poor by a multiplicity of factors. Africa as a continent is potentially endowed with rich natural and human resources. The question now is how the continent is working out of poverty so that the people experience, at least, some concrete glimpses of riches in their daily lives?

Also, it is a truism that Africans are religious and today the major religions in Africa are impacting on the lives of the people in a significant way from cradle to grave. On the one hand religion can be said to be helping in ameliorating poverty and on the other hand, it is used as an instrument of deepening the poverty status of the people. This places religion at the centre of both Africa's development and poverty. The writer therefore touches on the understanding of the three major religions in Africa of poverty and how the religious groups are trying to deal with this phenomenon of poverty. It is the hope that many people will gain from this work and contribute their quota to Africa's Renaissance.

List Price: $39.99
6" x 9"   (15.24 x 22.86 cm)
Number of pages: 204
ISBN-13:   978-1456367190
ISBN-10:   1456367196

Book found in:

    a.   https://www.createspace.com/3505215
    b.   http://www.amazon.de/s/ref=nb_sb_noss
?__mk_de_DE=%C5M%C5Z%D5%D1
&url=search-alias%3Daps&field-
keywords=eric+wiafe&x=0&y=0

Title: Christianity and African Traditional Religion's Approach to issues of Life and Death

Christianity and African Traditional Religion's Approach to Issues of Life and Death

Wissenschaft & Technik

Eric Kwabena Oduro Wiafe

Project Summary:

This study is concerned with the response that the Catholic Church, specifically the Catholic Archdiocese of Accra, is giving to the Akan

80

traditional concept of life and death. The focus group is the Akan of the Catholic Archdiocese of Accra.

The research revealed the difficult situation of Akan Catholics in the face of their Akan traditional practice. In some situations Akan Catholics have to make a choice between their Roman Catholic practice and their Akan traditional practice. An example is whether to go through the widowhood rites as required by Akan tradition or not. We also found in the research the importance that the Catholic Church, and for that matter the Catholic Archdiocese of Accra in particular, is giving to all these situations so as to help the people to conform to the beliefs and practices of the Church. This indicates the seriousness that the Church attaches to inculturation. The Church does not want to make the mistake of the past where some missionaries condemned everything African and tried to westernize Africans through religion. The Church acknowledges that the key to the growth and future of the Church in Africa is inculturation. In quoting Platvoet, Omenyo states that the Akan Traditional Religion is very accommodating, adaptable and highly dynamic (Omenyo, C. N., 2002). The Catholic Church, therefore, has to study the Akan traditional religion and explore all the possibilities to inculturate some of the beliefs and practices of Akan traditional religion so as to enhance her evangelizing mission.

In view of the above, this work attests to the responses that the Church has given to the various issues that were raised in the discussions, namely the issues of life and death.

The Church is doing something concrete on making Akan Catholics understand their faith and live by it. This becomes imperative when it comes to the issue of childbearing. On this issue Akans see barrenness as a problem, and so they are taught by the clergy and their lay collaborators the reasons for barrenness and the need to accept the will of God in their lives.

On the subject of death, the response of the Roman Catholic Church is mainly in teaching on the need for Christians to believe in the resurrection of Jesus Christ. The Catholic Archdiocese of Accra is responding to the various traditional death and funeral rituals, especially widowhood rites, and putting in place an alternative for Catholics in the Archdiocese of Accra. This is saving many women from the rigorous and inhuman treatment of widows (widowers).

The response of the Church makes her teachings and beliefs more meaningful and acceptable and thus enhances the Church's *growth in all aspects of her life.*

Year of Publication: 2010
Number of pages: 176
ISBN: 978-3-86624-512-9
PREMIUM
Publisher: dissertation.de - Verlag im Internet GmbH
Book Price: 43.90 EUR
PDF-Price: 26.12 EUR

Book found in:

1. http://www.dissertation.de/index.php3?active_document=buch.php3&sprache=2&buch=6137

Title: Towards a New Consciousness for a Better Africa: Some topical Issues in Ghana

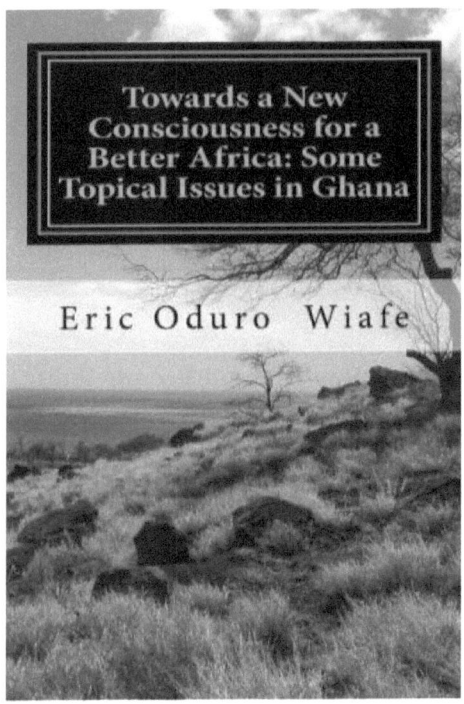

Project Summary

Africa's transformation and progress depend on Africans themselves. There is the need for a change of attitude and a strong desire to work towards a new Africa where the people have

84

much more peace and holistic development, so that they can contribute positively their quota to world development. The essays in this book look at the African situation and give suggestions as to what could be done to uplift the spirit of the people of Africa in their quest for freedom, peace and development.

Product Details

- **Paperback:** 134 pages
- **Date of Publication:** December 2010
- **Language:** English
- **ISBN-10:** 1456449710
- **ISBN-13:** 978-1456449711
- **Product Dimensions:** 8.5 x 5.5 x 0.3 inches

Book found here:
https://www.createspace.com/3525926

Title: Communicating Faith in Africa: The Ghanaian Experience

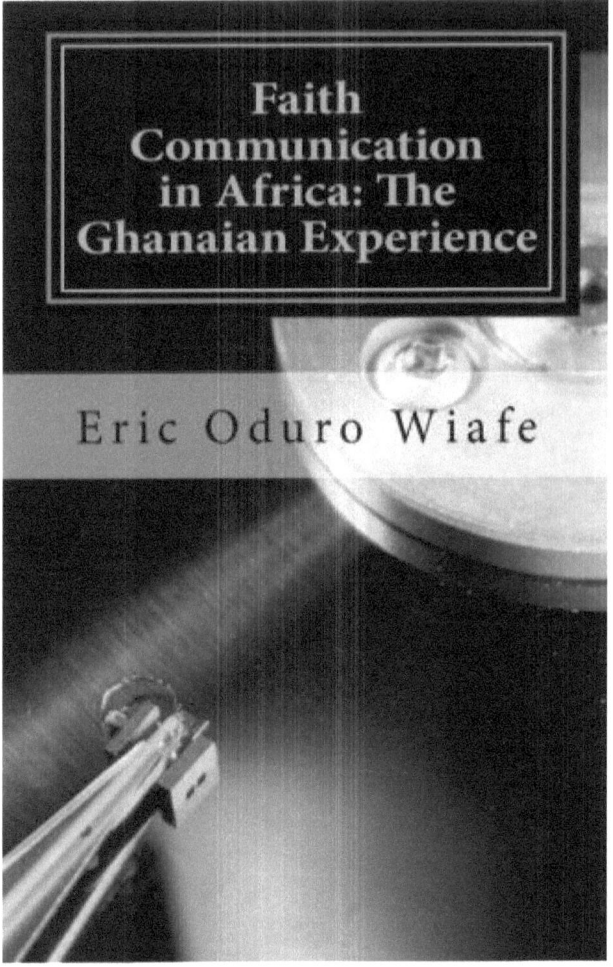

Project Summary

Faith Communication is not only relevant but an important commitment that every Christian is to make if we are to fulfill the mission Jesus Christ entrusted to us, that is, to go into the whole world and preach the gospel to every nation. This book looks at some of the African traditional ways of faith communication before the advent of European missionaries to Africa, South of the Sahara; the current means of faith communication and how to use the new communication technologies in disseminating the gospel of Jesus Christ and the teachings of the Church in our modern times. Some Churches are already applying these necessary communication tools in their work of evangelization in a rapidly growing and advancing world of science and technology, but much more work needs to be done, hence, this book on faith communication in Africa is timely.

List Price: $15.00
5.25" x 8" (13.335 x 20.32 cm)
Black & White on Cream paper
132 pages
ISBN-13: 978-1456472702
ISBN-10: 1456472704
BISAC: Religion / Christian Education / General

Summary of pages where one can order these books:

    a. https://www.createspace.com/3498839
    b. https://www.createspace.com/3505215
    c. http://www.amazon.de/s/ref=nb_sb_noss?__mk_de_DE=%C5M%C5Z%D5%D1&url=search-alias%3Daps&field-keywords=eric+wiafe&x=0&y=0
    d. http://www.dissertation.de/index.php3?active_document=buch.php3&sprache=2&buch=6137

Contact E-Mail address of Author, Rev. Fr. Dr. Eric Oduro Wiafe is, **frekow5@yahoo.com**